GLADIATORS

Natalie Hyde

CRABTREE
Publishing Company
www.crabtreebooks.com

Crabtree Publishing Company
www.crabtreebooks.com

Author: Natalie Hyde
**Publishing plan research
    and development**: Reagan Miller
Project coordinator: Crystal Sikkens
Editors: Sonya Newland, Crystal Sikkens
Proofreader: Janine Deschenes
Original design: Tim Mayer (Mayer Media)
Book design: Clare Nicholas
Cover design: Ken Wright
**Production coordinator and
    prepress technician**: Ken Wright
Print coordinator: Margaret Amy Salter
Production coordinated by: White-Thomson
Publishing

Photographs:
Alamy: North Wind Picture Archives: p. 8;
Moviestore collection Ltd: pp. 22–23; dieKleinert:
p. 25; The Print Collector: pp. 34–35; Bridgeman
Art Library: McBride, Angus (1931-2007) /
Private Collection / © Look and Learn: p. 40;
Corbis: National Geographic Creative: p. 9;
© Philcold/Dreamstime: cover; Stefano
Bianchetti: pp. 10–11, 38–39; Roger Wood: pp.
16–17; Araldo de Luca: p. 18; Bettmann: p. 37;
HO/Reuters: p. 42; Getty Images: Universal
History Archive: p. 27; iStock: ZU_09: p. 12; Craig
McCausland: p. 14; treeffe: p. 21; Ary6: p. 29;
Shutterstock: meirion Matthias: pp. 1, 44–45;
Iakov Kalinin: pp. 3, 30–31; nito: pp. 7, 36; Everett
Historical: p. 15; Bildagentur Zoonar GmbH: p.
17; R.A.R. de Bruijn Holding BV: p. 20; stemack:
p. 24; diak: pp. 28–29; Georgy Kuryatov: pp.
32–33; konstantinks: p. 41; riekephotos: p. 43;
Wikimedia: 26; Jean-Leon_Gerome_Pollice_Verso:
pp. 4–5; Marie-Lan Nguyen: p. 13; Jastrow: p. 19.

Library and Archives Canada Cataloguing in Publication

Hyde, Natalie, 1963-, author
    Gladiators / Natalie Hyde.

(Crabtree chrome)
Includes index.
Issued in print and electronic formats.
ISBN 978-0-7787-2288-5 (bound).--ISBN 978-0-7787-2227-4
(paperback).--ISBN 978-1-4271-8086-5 (html)

    1. Gladiators--Juvenile literature. I. Title. II. Series: Crabtree
chrome

GV35.H94 2016   j796.80937   C2015-907947-0
                                           C2015-907948-9

Library of Congress Cataloging-in-Publication Data

Names: Hyde, Natalie, 1963- author.
Title: Gladiators / Natalie Hyde.
Description: New York : Crabtree Publishing Company,
[2016] | Series: Crabtree chrome | Includes index. |
Description based on print version record and CIP data
provided by publisher; resource not viewed.
Identifiers: LCCN 2015045771 (print) | LCCN 2015045127
(ebook) | ISBN 9781427180865 (electronic HTML) | ISBN
9780778722885 (reinforced library binding : alk. paper) |
ISBN 9780778722274 (pbk. : alk. paper)
Subjects: LCSH: Gladiators--Rome--History--Juvenile
literature.
Classification: LCC GV35 (print) | LCC GV35 .H93 2016
(ebook) | DDC 796.80937--dc23
LC record available at http://lccn.loc.gov/2015045771

Crabtree Publishing Company

www.crabtreebooks.com   1-800-387-7650

Printed in Canada/022016/MA20151130

Published in Canada
Crabtree Publishing
616 Welland Ave.
St. Catharines, ON
L2M 5V6

Published in the United States
Crabtree Publishing
PMB 59051
350 Fifth Avenue, 59th Floor
New York, New York 10118

Published in the United Kingdom
Crabtree Publishing
Maritime House
Basin Road North, Hove
BN41 1WR

Published in Australia
Crabtree Publishing
3 Charles Street
Coburg North
VIC 3058

Contents

Roman Fighting Machines

Watch and Wait

Flamma slowly circled his opponent. Armed with only a short sword and a shield, he had to get in close to the enemy in order to strike. The two small eyeholes in his helmet made it hard to see. Flamma lunged left and felt the net thrown from his opponent slide off his round helmet.

◄ *Flamma fought in 34 fights in his time as a gladiator. He lost only four of them.*

4

Crowd Pleaser

Flamma jumped to the
right to avoid the **trident** jabbed at him. He stumbled but
managed to right himself. He struck his opponent fiercely
with his sword and the gladiator fell to the ground. The
crowd roared with pleasure. Flamma would fight another day.

Flamma was a *secutor*, or chaser. Chasers were
often paired with net throwers because they
used opposing tactics. The chaser needed to
get in close to strike. The net thrower needed
to stay back to use his long trident and net.

trident: a spear with three points

What Is a Gladiator?

Gladiators were warriors. They fought in **arenas** in ancient Rome. They were well fed and well trained. Some were even famous in Roman society. They were treated like rock stars. But not all gladiators came out of the arena alive. Gladiators knew this and were prepared to die.

▼ *Gladiator games took place all over the Roman Empire. This map shows how big the empire was around the second century C.E.*

Roman Empire, C.E. 117

Atlantic Ocean

North Sea

Caspian Sea

Black Sea

Rome ○ ITALY

Mediterranean Sea

Red Sea

0   1000 miles

0   1000 kilometers

Death in the Arena

Most gladiators thought their death would bring them glory. It was a chance to die with honor. Dying with honor meant you accepted your end without begging, yelling, or crying out in pain. Gladiators were even given special training in how to die this way.

> "I will endure to be burned, to be bound, to be beaten, and to be killed by the sword."
>
> Gladiator oath

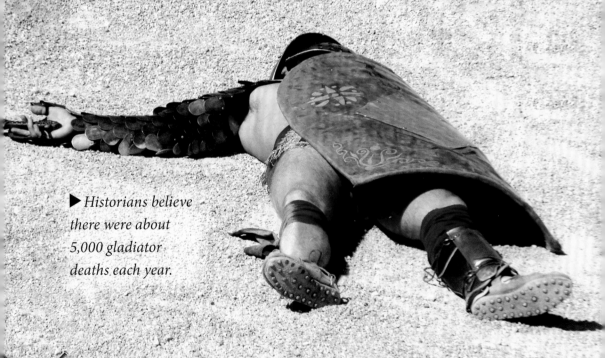

▶ Historians believe there were about 5,000 gladiator deaths each year.

arenas: large open areas where competitions are held

7

The Criminal Class

Gladiators came from many different parts of society. Where they came from determined the type of battle they would fight. Serious criminals were the lowest group. This included people who had committed murder and **arson**. They often had to fight men or wild animals without weapons. They were not expected to live.

▼ *Criminals often had to fight wild beasts instead of other gladiators.*

"In the morning, men are thrown to lions and bears. At midday, they are thrown to the spectators themselves. No sooner has a man killed, than they shout for him to kill another."

Roman philosopher Seneca, describing how criminals were treated in the arena

Sent to School

Slaves who had committed crimes were sent to gladiator schools as punishment. They joined prisoners of war to be trained as warriors. Some free men volunteered to be gladiators. They often had the best weapons and armor. They also fought the weakest challengers, so they had a good chance of winning.

▼ *A family could sell a slave to a gladiator school if he disobeyed them.*

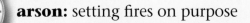

arson: setting fires on purpose

Sort Them Out

There were different types of gladiators, and they used different weapons and methods of fighting. Some, called the *essedarius*, rode on **chariots** and used spears or swords as their weapons. Others fought on horseback and used long swords to reach their enemy. Some were on foot and had two swords—one in each hand.

▼ *The* bestiarii, *or beast fighters, were the group of gladiators that fought wild animals such as elephants and lions.*

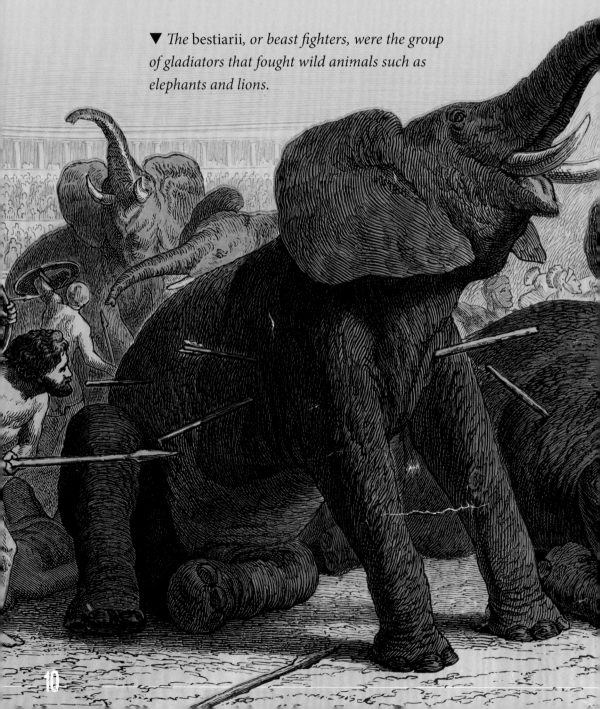

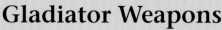

Gladiator Weapons

Almost any kind of object could be used as a weapon. Some gladiators used ropes thrown in a loop, called lassos. Some used a bow and arrow. Other fighters used a trident, knife, or net.

Sometimes, two gladiators would fight and then the winner would fight a third gladiator, known as a *tertiarius*. A *tertiarius* could also be used as a backup in a regular two-man combat, if another gladiator could not fight.

chariots: two-wheeled carts pulled by horses

Fighting Emperors

Emperors were the leaders in ancient Rome. They paid for and staged many of the gladiator games. The games included the deaths of criminals, animal fights, and the gladiator combats. Sometimes, an emperor wanted to join in the fighting. He wore full body armor and fought only weaker challengers.

▲ *Emperors often fought from the safety of a chariot so they would not get hurt, but some fought on foot.*

Out of Control

Commodus became Roman Emperor in 180 C.E. He wanted fame and glory, and was determined to be a gladiator. In the morning he would hunt and kill beasts in the arena. In the afternoon he would fight gladiators. His actions became so extreme that his advisers thought he was too dangerous to lead the Roman empire. So, they had him killed.

Most Romans thought Commodus was a joke as a gladiator. The emperor had to pay people to call out *compliments* from the seats.

▶*Commodus believed that he had been the great warrior Hercules in a former life.*

compliments: words of praise

Duty or Fun?

Honor and Respect

The gladiator games did not start out as **entertainment**. They were a way for people to honor a dead relative. Slaves would fight to the death on the day of the funeral. This special event was called a *munerus*.

▼ All Romans— free or slaves—were buried outside city limits. This was so the dead did not pollute their community.

The famous roman leader, Julius Caesar, honored his father with 320 pairs of gladiators dressed in silver armor.

Bigger is Better?

The first *munerus* took place in 264 B.C.E. The sons of Junius Brutus Pera organized an event in which three pairs of slaves fought each other. It was not long before *munera* became the most popular part of funerals. Soon, the rich and powerful citizens were trying to outdo each other.

▼ *The first* munerus *was held at a place known as the Forum Boarium. Parts of it are still standing today.*

entertainment: something that is done for fun

How to Win Votes

Originally, the family of the dead person paid for the gladiator fights. Over time, politicians, or elected officials, began hosting *munera* to win over the crowds and earn votes. They began using money from the public's **taxes** to pay for bigger and bigger *munera*.

Around 106 C.E., Emperor Trajan won a war with the Dacian people, who lived near the Black Sea in Europe. Trajan celebrated with games lasting 123 days. He used 10,000 gladiators and 11,000 animals.

▼ *As the games got larger, more and more animals were used. So many animals were killed that some species, such as the North African elephant, were completely wiped out.*

Setting Limits

People began to get angry that their taxes were being spent in this way. The Roman emperor Augustus created new laws. He narrowed down who could host a *munerus*. He stated how many times a year they could take place. He also limited how many gladiators could take part.

▶ *Emperor Augustus stopped certain people from taking part in the gladiator games, including important members of government.*

taxes: the money people pay to a government to help run a country

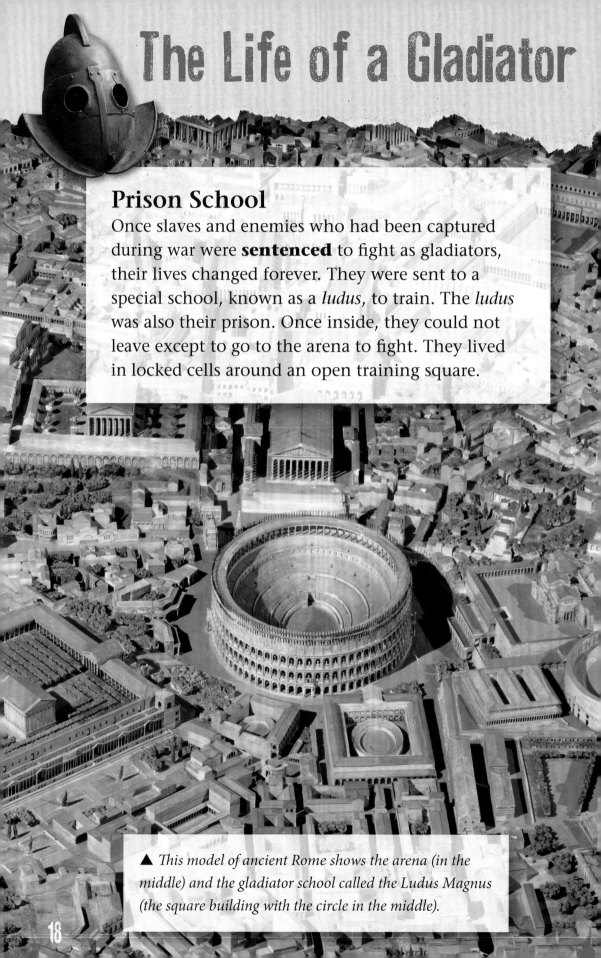

The Life of a Gladiator

Prison School

Once slaves and enemies who had been captured during war were **sentenced** to fight as gladiators, their lives changed forever. They were sent to a special school, known as a *ludus*, to train. The *ludus* was also their prison. Once inside, they could not leave except to go to the arena to fight. They lived in locked cells around an open training square.

▲ *This model of ancient Rome shows the arena (in the middle) and the gladiator school called the Ludus Magnus (the square building with the circle in the middle).*

Ready to Fight

The *ludus* was controlled by a *lanista*, or manager. He decided when and where the gladiators would fight. Gladiators were expected to fight two or three times a year. The *lanista* made sure the gladiators were well looked after. He needed them to stay strong so they would survive in the arena.

▼ *The remains of the biggest gladiator school, the Ludus Magnus, can still be seen in Rome today.*

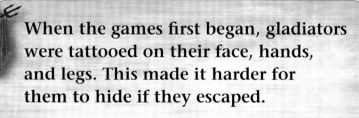

When the games first began, gladiators were tattooed on their face, hands, and legs. This made it harder for them to hide if they escaped.

sentenced: stated the punishment for something

Train With Me

When the new gladiators arrived, the *lanista* and a doctor would examine them. The type of gladiator they would be, and the kind of training they received, depended on their body type and health. Trainers were often **retired** gladiators.

▲ *Gladiators using the same kind of weapons would train together.*

Learning to Be the Best

Gladiators trained every day. Many people visited the *ludi* to see the training when there were no games. The gladiators used wooden weapons to practice so they would not get hurt, but it was still exciting to watch.

The Ludus Magnus in Rome had an underground tunnel that linked it directly to the huge arena called the Colosseum. The gladiators would march through the tunnel, knowing that some of them would not march back again at the end of the day's fighting.

▼ *This is the palestra, or training ground, at Pompeii in Italy, where gladiators would live and practice.*

retired: no longer working

What to Wear?

Different types of gladiators wore different armor. They trained and fought with the same armor and weapons all the time. Some gladiators had heavy armor, including metal breastplates, large shields, and helmets. Light armor included leather arm and leg protectors, and a light helmet. The worst criminals had no protection at all.

Mostly Bare

Gladiators did not wear much clothing. Heavily armored fighters wore close-fitting linen clothes under their metal armor so it would not rub against their skin. Light or unarmored fighters wore only a cloth around their waist, called a loincloth. Horseback fighters would wear a **tunic**. All gladiators wore sandals or went barefoot.

◀ *Almost all gladiators fought with a bare chest. Romans thought this showed strength.*

Gladiators used different kinds of shields. Smaller, lighter ones were round. A larger, rectangular one, called a *scutum*, was used by heavily armored gladiators.

tunic: a loose, sleeveless garment that reached down to the knees

Sword or Knife?

There were many kinds of weapons used by gladiators. The weapons they used identified the type of gladiator that was fighting. Some gladiators fought with swords. Swords could be curved or straight and long or short. A long spear, called a lance, was often used by fighters on horseback. Other gladiators used short knives called daggers, whips, or **clubs**.

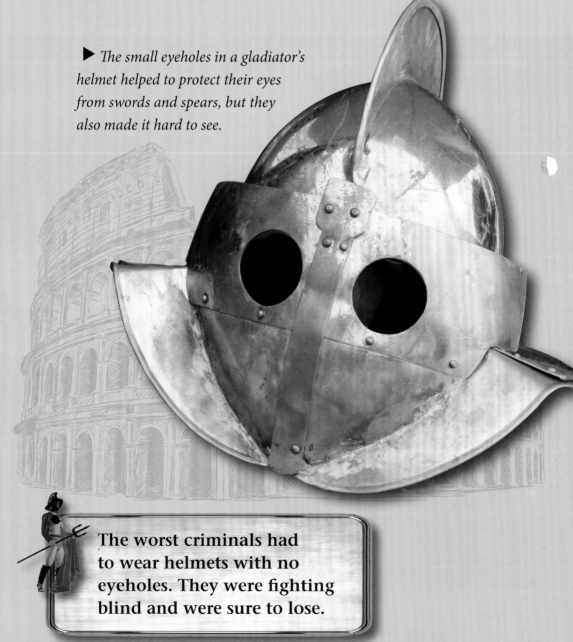

▶ *The small eyeholes in a gladiator's helmet helped to protect their eyes from swords and spears, but they also made it hard to see.*

The worst criminals had to wear helmets with no eyeholes. They were fighting blind and were sure to lose.

A Fair Fight

Pairs of gladiators rarely had the same weapons or armor.
Crowds liked to see a heavily armed fighter against a lighter
one. They thought it made the fight more interesting.
The heavily armed fighter was better protected but
he could not move easily. The lightly armored fighter
could move quickly, but had little protection.

▼ *Stronger, more experienced, or better-armored
gladiators often fought weaker ones.*

clubs: heavy wooden sticks used as weapons

25

Female Gladiators

Romans were always looking for something new and interesting in the games. So, when female gladiators were fighting, it was a special event. Women fighters were called gladiatrices. Most were slaves, but some were wealthy women who may have fought for the excitement and fame.

▲ *Women usually fought other women rather than men or animals, but sometimes they fought as venatores—beast-hunters.*

"**Emperor Domitian gave... gladiatorial shows at night by the light of torches, and not only combats between men but between women as well.**"

Roman historian, Suetonius

Nice Do!

Gladiatrices were treated almost the same as men in the games. A stone carving in Turkey shows two women fighting. They are wearing only loincloths with belts. They are carrying short knives and holding shields. The biggest difference is that the women are not wearing helmets. Some think this was so the crowd could see the woman's hairstyle and better identify the gladiator's **gender**.

▼ *This carving was made to celebrate the freeing of two female gladiators, Amazon and Achilia. They may have earned their freedom by showing the crowd a fight of skill and bravery.*

gender: whether someone is male or female

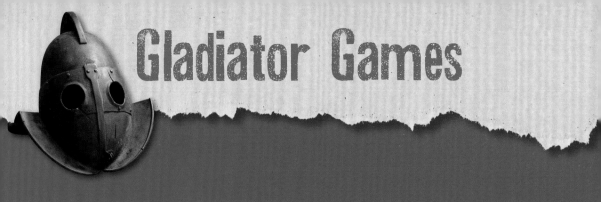

Gladiator Games

Meet Me at the Forum

The first *munera* were not held in arenas. Gladiators performed in an open town square called a forum. Forums were normally used as market places. Sometimes the **stalls** got in the way of people seeing the action. There also was not enough seating for the crowds. As the games got bigger, they needed a better place to hold them.

▼ *These pillars are the remains of a covered walkway in this ancient forum. If it was raining, the market stalls would be under it. On nice days, they would be set up in the square.*

The floor of an amphitheater was covered with sand to soak up any blood. Sand is called *harena* in Latin, which is where the name "arena" comes from.

If You Build It, They Will Come

Amphitheaters were soon built in Rome to hold these shows. They were round or oval shaped, with layers of seating all the way around. The first amphitheaters for *munera* were made of wood. Many of these burned down. Later they were built with stone.

▲ *The oldest stone amphitheater is in Pompeii. It seated 20,000 people.*

stalls: booths for selling things

The Colosseum

The Colosseum in Rome was the most famous amphitheater. The first games held there were in 80 C.E. The Colosseum had four levels of seating and was as tall as a 12-story building today. It could seat 50,000 people. Pillars were placed around the top level. These held up an **awning** so the crowds could sit in the shade.

▲ *Emperor Titus opened the Colosseum with 100 days of games. Around 9,000 animals were killed in hunts and fights.*

Down Under

The floor of the arena had 36 trapdoors. Through them, gladiators or animals could rise from the ground like magic. Underneath the floor was a maze of tunnels, ramps, animal cages, and rooms to hold gladiators and criminals sentenced to death. There were also tunnels so the emperor could avoid the crowds.

Under the Colosseum floor were around 60 machines to lift animals and scenery up to the arena floor. Each one needed eight men to turn the handles to lift the cages up two stories.

awning: a sheet of material stretched on a frame to make shade

Take a Seat

The games were free, but people had tickets that showed their seat number. A person sat according to their importance. The emperor sat at one end of the arena at ground level. Knights and wealthy people sat in the next level up. Ordinary citizens sat in the rows above them. The very top level was left for the poor, slaves, and women.

Get Your Program Here!

Billboards around the city advertised the event. People could buy programs to see which gladiators were fighting that day. The games lasted all day. Some people brought lunch and ate it in their seats. Others left the arena to buy water, wine, or stuffed pastries from vendors.

▼ *The top-level seats in the amphitheater were a long way from the action.*

People had to get their tickets for the games well in advance. If a person was not able to get a free ticket, they could buy a seat from a *scalper* on the day of the games, but often for a high price.

scalper: someone who resells tickets at a higher price

A Day at the Games

Games day opened with a parade. It started with wild animals led by trainers. Then came dancers, acrobats, and hunters. Last came the gladiators holding their weapons. The morning events might include animal hunts or even sea battles. To perform sea battles, the floor of the arena was flooded with water.

> **"We who are about to die, salute you!"**
>
> Gladiator's salute to the emperor as they entered the arena

▶ *Gladiators saluted the emperor before the fight began.*

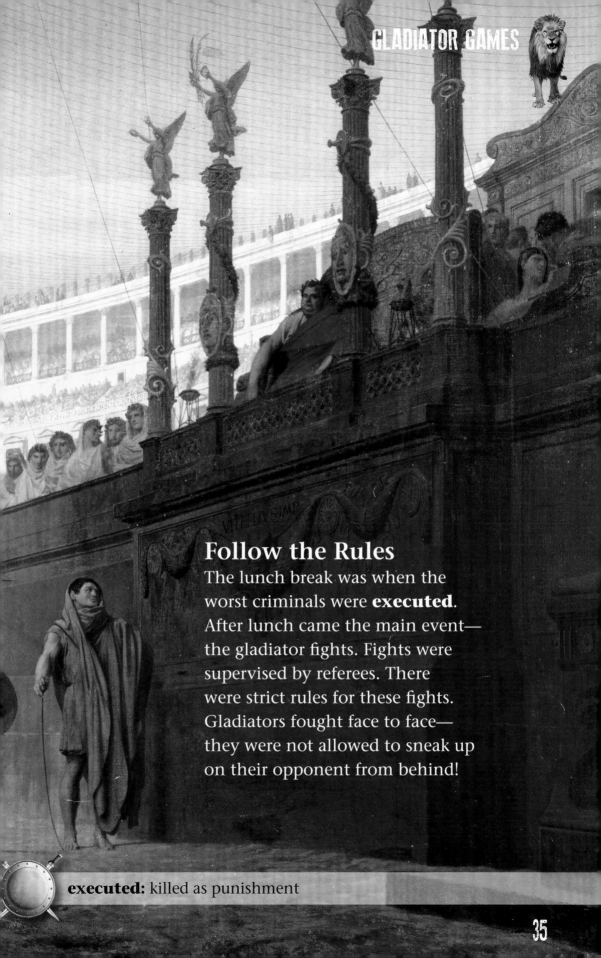

Follow the Rules

The lunch break was when the worst criminals were **executed**. After lunch came the main event—the gladiator fights. Fights were supervised by referees. There were strict rules for these fights. Gladiators fought face to face—they were not allowed to sneak up on their opponent from behind!

executed: killed as punishment

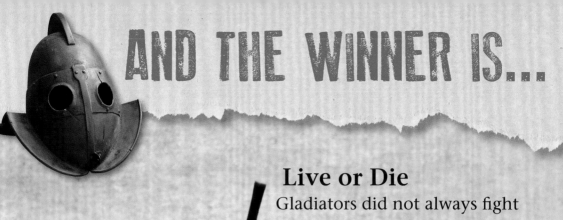

Live or Die

Gladiators did not always fight to the death. They were expensive to house, feed, and train, so their managers wanted them around for many fights! Volunteers and emperors who wanted to take part in the games were given special treatment so they would not get hurt.

▲ *Often gladiator fights would end in a tie.*

Mercy, Please!

Sometimes one fighter would get injured. If he wanted to beg for **mercy** he could raise a finger, often on his left hand. Depending on how well the gladiator fought, and if he or she pleased the crowd, the emperor would turn his thumb a certain way to show whether he wanted the gladiator to live or die.

▼ *The emperor usually had the last word on whether a gladiator would live or die.*

Our "thumbs up" and "thumbs down" sign began from the gladiatorial games. Some fights during the games were listed as *sine missione*, which means "without mercy." This meant the fight would be to the death.

mercy: to be forgiven instead of punished

Survival

It was possible for some gladiators to earn their freedom in the arena. Slaves who were very skilled or brave during a fight might be set free. During some periods of Roman history, gladiators could earn their freedom by winning five fights.

▲ *Slaves were thought to be property. A* lanista *would buy slaves that he thought were strong and fit to be trained as gladiators.*

Freedom!

A freed slave was called a *rudiarius*. He was given a wooden sword called a *rudis* in a special **ceremony**. Afterward, he could retire or work as a bodyguard or referee. He could also work as a trainer in a gladiator school. Flamma was offered his *rudis* four times. He turned it down each time and continued to fight.

Even when a slave was freed, he was not allowed to become a Roman citizen. However, a slave's children could be citizens of Rome.

ceremony: a formal event

39

The Story of Spartacus

Spartacus was a soldier who was captured and sold into slavery. He trained as a gladiator, but disliked his trainer. He convinced 70 other slaves to break free and escape with him. He fought against the Romans for two years, with an army of slaves from the countryside. Spartacus was eventually killed fighting the Roman army.

▼ *Spartacus was at the front of the attack in the final battle near the Sele River. Witnesses said he died there, but his body was never found.*

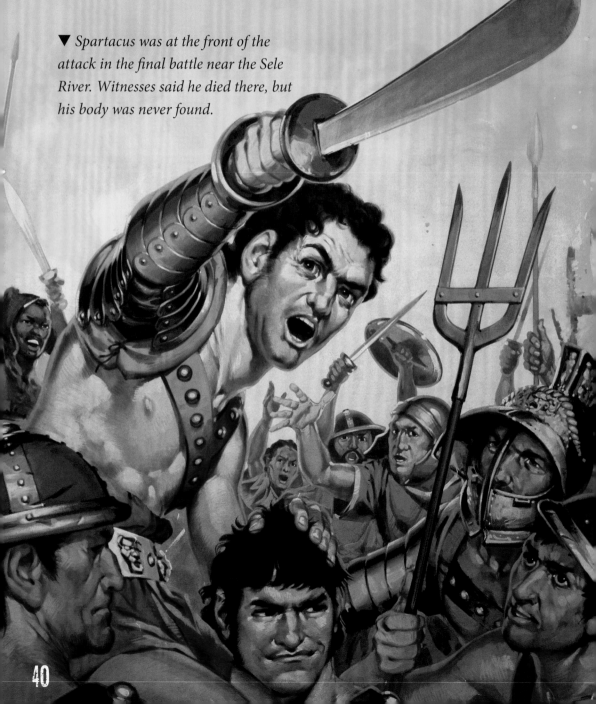

40

Let's Call it a Draw

Priscus and Verus were two **rival** gladiators. Their big fight on opening day of the Colosseum lasted for hours. They both gave up at the same time and laid down their swords together to show respect for each other. The crowds cheered. Emperor Titus awarded them each a *rudis*. They left the arena as free men.

▶ *Emperor Titus hosted the very first games that took place at the Colosseum.*

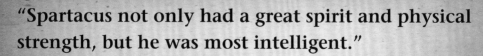

"Spartacus not only had a great spirit and physical strength, but he was most intelligent."

Plutarch, writing about Spartacus

rival: a person competing against you

Houses of the Dead

About one million gladiators died in the arenas. After the fight, their bodies were taken back to a room where their armor and weapons were removed. These were given back to their *lanista*. Gladiators were thought to have a lower **status** than other people, even in death. Some were buried outside the city in mass graves. Others, often criminals with a death sentence, were sometimes thrown in a river.

▲ *Scientists studied the skeletons found in a gladiator graveyard. They learned a lot about the life, health, and death of gladiators.*

It is said that dead criminals were fed to the animals used in gladiator fights. This gave them the taste for human flesh so they would attack more.

Gladiator Graveyards

Free men who volunteered for gladiator games were treated with respect after they died. Their families gave them a proper burial. But they were still often buried in separate cemeteries. Gladiators who died with honor were sometimes buried with items such as the remains of a feast, pottery, and lamps. It was thought these items would help them in their life after death.

▶ *Gravestones often gave interesting information about a gladiator's life. One mentioned that the gladiator had died because the referee made a bad call!*

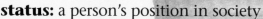

status: a person's position in society

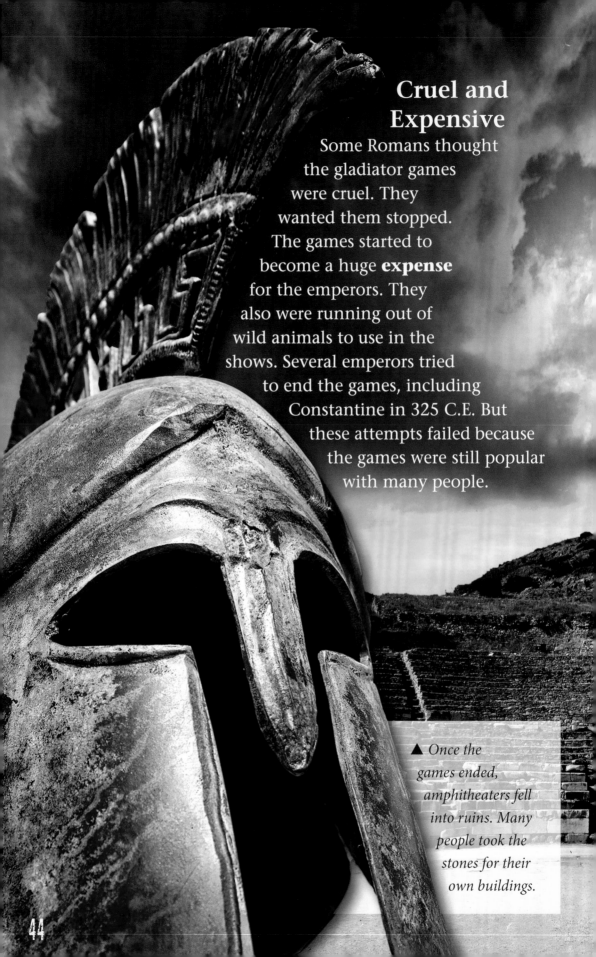

Cruel and Expensive

Some Romans thought the gladiator games were cruel. They wanted them stopped. The games started to become a huge **expense** for the emperors. They also were running out of wild animals to use in the shows. Several emperors tried to end the games, including Constantine in 325 C.E. But these attempts failed because the games were still popular with many people.

▲ *Once the games ended, amphitheaters fell into ruins. Many people took the stones for their own buildings.*

The End

Finally a religious man named Telemachus took action. At one of the games, he stepped down into the arena to break up a gladiator fight. The crowd was angry that their fun was ruined. They stoned him to death. Emperor Honorius was horrified by what happened to Telemachus. He officially banned the games in 404 C.E.

People are still fascinated by the lives and deaths of gladiators. Around the world, people dress as gladiators and act out battles in arenas. The Colosseum in Rome is one of the most popular tourist attractions in the world.

expense: the amount of money something costs

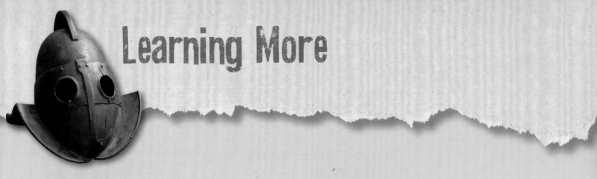

Learning More

Books

The Gladiator's Victory
by Benjamin Hulme-Cross
(Crabtree, 2015)

You Wouldn't Want to be a Roman Gladiator!
by John Malam
(Franklin Watts, 2012)

Gladiators: 100 BC–AD 200
by Stephen Wisdom
(Osprey Publishing, 2001)

Gladiator
by Richard Watkins
(HMH Books, 2000)

The Roman Colosseum
by Elizabeth Mann
(Wonders of the World, 2006)

Life as a Gladiator
by Michael Burgan
(Capstone, 2010)

Websites

http://rome.mrdonn.org/gladiators.html
Explore ancient Rome with this ancient civilization for kids.

www.ducksters.com/history/ancient_roman_arena_entertainment.php
Ducksters talks about the arena and entertainment in ancient Rome.

www.ducksters.com/history/ancient_rome/spartacus.php
All about the famous gladiator, Spartacus.

www.historyforkids.net/roman-gladiators.html
History for Kids takes a look at Roman gladiators.

www.kidinfo.com/world_history/ancient_rome.html
A great portal for links about all things Roman, including gladiators.

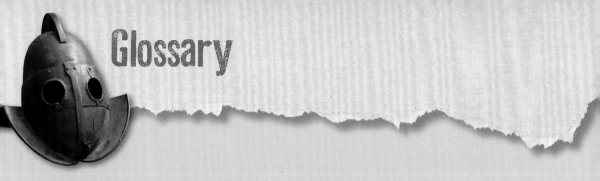

Glossary

arenas Large open areas where competitions are held

arson Setting fires on purpose

awning A sheet of material stretched on a frame to make shade

ceremony A formal event

chariots Two-wheeled carts pulled by horses

clubs Heavy wooden sticks used as a weapon

compliments Words of praise

entertainment Something that is done for fun

executed Killed as punishment

expense The amount of money something costs

gender Whether someone is male or female

mercy To be forgiven instead of punished

retired No longer working

rival A person competing against you

scalper Someone who resells tickets at a higher price

sentenced Stated the punishment for something

stalls Booths for selling things

status A person's position in society

taxes The money people pay to a government to help run a country

trident A spear with three points

tunic A loose, sleeveless garment that reached down to the knees

Index

Entries in **bold** refer to pictures